**TREETOPS CLAS**

# Stage 16 Pack A
# Teaching Notes

*Jo Tregenza*

**OXFORD**
UNIVERSITY PRESS

# Contents

| | |
|---|---|
| Introduction | 4 |
| Comprehension strategies | 5 |
| Cross-curricular links | 6 |
| Curriculum coverage chart | 7 |

## Frankenstein

| | |
|---|---|
| Synopsis | 10 |
| Group or guided reading | 11 |
| Speaking, listening and drama activities | 12 |
| Writing activities | 13 |

## Jane Eyre

| | |
|---|---|
| Synopsis | 14 |
| Group or guided reading | 15 |
| Speaking, listening and drama activities | 16 |
| Writing activities | 17 |

## Stories of Sherlock Holmes

| | |
|---|---|
| Synopsis | 18 |
| Group or guided reading | 19 |
| Speaking, listening and drama activities | 20 |
| Writing activities | 20 |

## Wuthering Heights
| | |
|---|---|
| Synopsis | 22 |
| Group or guided reading | 22 |
| Speaking, listening and drama activities | 24 |
| Writing activities | 24 |

## Treasure Island
| | |
|---|---|
| Synopsis | 26 |
| Group or guided reading | 27 |
| Speaking, listening and drama activities | 28 |
| Writing activities | 29 |

## Robinson Crusoe
| | |
|---|---|
| Synopsis | 30 |
| Group or guided reading | 30 |
| Speaking, listening and drama activities | 32 |
| Writing activities | 32 |

# Introduction

*TreeTops* Classics are abridged versions of classic texts especially chosen to appeal to 9–11 year olds. They are ideal for use in group sessions and as model texts for writing. They are also an excellent stimulus for other writing activities and for speaking and listening.

*TreeTops* Stages follow on from the Oxford Reading Tree Stages and are designed to be used flexibly, matched to individual pupils' reading ability.

## How to introduce the books

Before reading the book, read the title and the blurb on the back cover. Ask the children what they think will happen. Read the authors' names (both original author and adapter) and talk about books by the same authors that the children may know. Look through the book briefly to find pictures of the main characters and discover the setting for the story.

Complete the reading session with the pupils telling you what they enjoyed about the story, encouraging them to refer to the text to support their reasons.

## Using this Teaching Notes booklet

These Teaching Notes provide guidance for using the book with groups of pupils or with individuals. Suggestions are provided for group or guided reading, speaking, listening and drama, writing and cross-curricular links. The activities largely focus on strategies to increase comprehension. Skills such as prediction, questioning, clarifying, summarising and imagining (see the comprehension strategies grid on page 5) are covered within the activities in these Teaching Notes. Repeatedly practising these skills will enhance children's ability to comprehend new texts when they meet them. The notes also include vocabulary enrichment activities (a key part of improving comprehension).

The cross-curricular links on page 6 provide a specific subject or thematic focus for each book, which can be further explored in the other *TreeTops* Classics titles listed in the chart.

In order to help your planning and record keeping, the curriculum coverage chart on pages 7–9 provides curriculum information relating to the curricula for England, Wales, Northern Ireland and Scotland. This includes PNS Literacy Framework objectives, Assessment Focuses and the reading, writing and speaking and listening levels children can reasonably be expected to be achieving when reading these *TreeTops* books.

## Notes for adults in *TreeTops* Classics books

Included on the inside covers of the pupil books are notes to help parents/carers or classroom assistants share the books with children.

## Comprehension strategies

| Book Title | Comprehension strategy taught through these Teaching Notes | | | | |
|---|---|---|---|---|---|
| | Prediction | Questioning | Clarifying | Summarising | Imagining |
| Frankenstein | ✓ | ✓ | ✓ | ✓ | ✓ |
| Jane Eyre | ✓ | ✓ | ✓ | ✓ | ✓ |
| Stories of Sherlock Holmes | ✓ | ✓ | ✓ | ✓ | |
| Wuthering Heights | ✓ | ✓ | ✓ | ✓ | ✓ |
| Treasure Island | ✓ | ✓ | ✓ | | ✓ |
| Robinson Crusoe | ✓ | | ✓ | ✓ | ✓ |

# Cross-curricular links

| *TreeTops* Classics Stage 16 Pack A | Cross-curricular links | Other TreeTops titles with similar links |
|---|---|---|
| Frankenstein | **Citizenship:** Developing good relationships and respecting the differences between people: 4a<br>**Science 4: Physical processes:** Electricity: 1b | *Jane Eyre* |
| Jane Eyre | **Citizenship:** Developing good relationships and respecting the differences between people: 4a, 4c<br>**History:** British history: 8a | *Frankenstein*<br><br>*Stories of Sherlock Holmes*<br>*Dr Jekyll and Mr Hyde* (Classics Stage 16 Pack B) |
| Stories of Sherlock Holmes | **Citizenship:** Preparing to play an active role as citizens: 2b<br>**History:** British history: 8a | *Jane Eyre*<br>*Dr Jekyll and Mr Hyde* (Classics Stage 16 Pack B) |
| Wuthering Heights | **Geography:** Knowledge and understanding of places: 3f<br>**History:** Knowledge and understanding of events, people and changes in the past: 2a | *Kidnapped* (Classics Stage 16 Pack B) |
| Treasure Island | **Geography:** Geography enquiry and skills: 2e<br>**History:** Britain and the wider world in Tudor times: 10 | *Robinson Crusoe*<br><br>*Robinson Crusoe*<br>*The Tempest* (Classics Stage 16 Pack B) |
| Robinson Crusoe | **Geography:** Geography enquiry and skills: 2e<br>**History:** Britain and the wider world in Tudor times: 10 | *Treasure Island*<br><br>*Treasure Island*<br>*The Tempest* (Classics Stage 16 Pack B) |

# Curriculum coverage chart

|  | Speaking, listening, drama | Reading | Writing |
|---|---|---|---|
| **Frankenstein** | | | |
| PNS Literacy Framework (Y6) | 4.1 | **V C** 7.2 | 9.2 |
| National Curriculum | Level 4/5 | Level 4/5<br>AF 2, 3 | Level 4/5<br>AF 1, 7 |
| Scotland (P7)<br>(5–14)<br>C for E | Within Level E<br>Second level | Within Level E<br>Second level | Within Level E<br>Second level |
| N. Ireland (P7/Y7) | 1, 2, 3, 4, 7, 11 | 1, 2, 3, 4, 9 | 1, 4, 6 |
| Wales (Y6) | Skills: 1, 2, 3<br>Range: 3, 4, 5 | Skills: 1, 2, 3, 5<br>Range: 1, 2, 3, 4 | Skills: 1, 4<br>Range: 1, 2, 3, 4 |
| **Jane Eyre** | | | |
| PNS Literacy Framework (Y6) | 4.1 | **V C** 8.3 | 9.4 |
| National Curriculum | Level 4/5 | Level 4/5<br>AF 5 | Level 4/5<br>AF 7 |
| Scotland (P7)<br>(5–14)<br>C for E | Within Level E<br>Second level | Within Level E<br>Second level | Within Level E<br>Second level |
| N. Ireland (P7/Y7) | 1, 3, 7, 8, 15 | 1, 2, 3, 4, 9 | 1, 4, 5, 6 |
| Wales (Y6) | Skills: 1, 2, 3, 4, 6, 7<br>Range: 2, 3, 4, 5, 6, 7, 8 | Skills: 1, 2, 3, 5, 7<br>Range: 1, 2, 3, 4 | Skills: 1, 2, 4, 6, 7<br>Range: 1, 2, 3, 4 |

**C** = Language comprehension   **V** = Vocabulary enrichment
**AF** = Assessment Focus   Y = Year   P = Primary

# Curriculum coverage chart

|  | Speaking, listening, drama | Reading | Writing |
|---|---|---|---|
| **Stories of Sherlock Holmes** | | | |
| PNS Literacy Framework (Y6) | 1.3 | **V C** 7.1 | 10.1 |
| National Curriculum | Level 4/5 | Level 4/5 AF 4, 6 | Level 4/5 AF 3 |
| Scotland (P7) (5–14) C for E | Within Level E Second level | Within Level E Second level | Within Level E Second level |
| N. Ireland (P7/Y7) | 1, 2, 3, 4, 5, 7, 11 | 1, 2, 3, 4, 6, 9, 12 | 1, 4, 5, 6, 7, 9 |
| Wales (Y6) | Skills: 1, 2, 3, 4 Range: 2, 3, 4, 5, 8 | Skills: 1, 2, 3, 4, 5, 7 Range: 1, 2, 3, 4 | Skills: 1, 2, 3, 4, 5, 6, 7, 8, 9 Range: 1, 2, 3, 4 |
| **Wuthering Heights** | | | |
| PNS Literacy Framework (Y6) | 3.1 | **V C** 7.2 | 9.2 |
| National Curriculum | Level 4/5 | Level 4/5 AF 2, 3 | Level 4/5 AF 1 |
| Scotland (P7) (5–14) C for E | Within Level E Second level | Within Level E Second level | Within Level E Second level |
| N. Ireland (P7/Y7) | 1, 2, 3, 4, 5, 6, 7, 8, 9, 10, 13 | 1, 2, 4, 5, 7, 9, 12 | 1, 4, 5, 6, 7 |
| Wales (Y6) | Skills: 1, 2, 3, 4, 6 Range: 2, 3, 4, 5, 8 | Skills: 1, 2, 3, 4, 5, 7 Range: 1, 2, 3, 4 | Skills: 1, 2, 3, 4, 5, 6, 7, 8 Range: 1, 2, 3, 4 |

**C** = Language comprehension   **V** = Vocabulary enrichment
**AF** = Assessment Focus   Y = Year   P = Primary

# Curriculum coverage chart

|  | Speaking, listening, drama | Reading | Writing |
|---|---|---|---|
| **Treasure Island** | | | |
| PNS Literacy Framework (Y6) | 2.1 | **V** **C** 7.3 | 9.2 |
| National Curriculum | Level 4/5 | Level 4/5 AF 4 | Level 4/5 AF 1 |
| Scotland (P7) (5–14) C for E | Within Level E Second level | Within Level E Second level | Within Level E Second level |
| N. Ireland (P7/Y7) | 1, 2, 5, 6 | 1, 2, 3, 4, 6, 9, 11 | 1, 4, 5, 6 |
| Wales (Y6) | Skills: 1 Range: 2, 4 | Skills: 1, 2, 3, 5, 7 Range: 1, 2, 3, 4 | Skills: 1, 2, 3, 4, 5, 6, 8 Range: 1, 2, 3, 4 |
| **Robinson Crusoe** | | | |
| PNS Literacy Framework (Y6) | 1.2 | **V** **C** 8.3 | 10.2 |
| National Curriculum | Level 4/5 | Level 4/5 AF 3, 4 | Level 4/5 AF 3 |
| Scotland (P7) (5–14) C for E | Within Level E Second level | Within Level E Second level | Within Level E Second level |
| N. Ireland (P7/Y7) | 1, 3, 4, 5, 7, 11, 13 | 1, 2, 3, 4, 5, 6, 9, 10 | 1, 2, 4, 5, 6 |
| Wales (Y6) | Skills: 1, 2, 3, 4 Range: 2, 3, 4, 5, 8 | Skills: 1, 2, 3, 4, 5, 7 Range: 1, 2, 3, 4 | Skills: 1, 2, 3, 4, 5, 6, 7 Range: 1, 2, 3, 4 |

**C** = Language comprehension    **V** = Vocabulary enrichment
AF = Assessment Focus    Y = Year   P = Primary

# Frankenstein

**Author:** Mary Shelley (1797–1851)

**Synopsis:** Victor Frankenstein is a scientist who becomes obsessed with the idea of creating life. His experiments lead him to make a living being, but he is disgusted by the ugliness of his creature. Frankenstein flees, leaving his monster to fend for itself. The monster becomes lonely and bitter when others find him repulsive and treat him cruelly. He becomes angry and causes the death of all those closest to Frankenstein. The story ends with Frankenstein dying of exhaustion after a long hunt for his monster, and the monster, upon hearing of his master's death, ends his own life.

**Social and historical context:** Mary Shelley was born in London in 1797 to parents who were well known philosophers and writers. When Mary was 17, she fell in love with the famous romantic poet Percy Bysshe Shelley (who she later married in 1818). In 1816, Mary, Percy and a few others went on holiday to Lake Geneva to stay with the poet Lord Byron. It was Lord Byron who challenged the group to write a ghost story. Mary had a nightmare and got the idea for a 'monster story', which was published two years later, when she was 21 years old. In the novel, Mary did not give the monster a name. It later became a common misconception that the name of the monster in Shelley's novel was Frankenstein, after the release of the film of the same name in the 1930s.

---

**C** = Language comprehension  **R, AF** = Reading Assessment Focus
**V** = Vocabulary enrichment  **W, AF** = Writing Assessment Focus

# Group or guided reading

## Introducing the book

**(C)** *(Clarifying, Prediction)* Tell the children the title of the book - *Frankenstein*. What images does it conjure up? Without showing the children the cover, ask them to draw what they think the monster looks like. Compare their drawings with the front cover.

**(C)** *(Clarifying)* Read up to the end of page 14 to the children. Ask them what they notice about the style of the two chapters. Who is the narrator of each? What is the impact of the change of narrator?

**(C)** *(Questioning)* Ask the children to generate their own questions about what they would like to ask the scientist Victor Frankenstein.

- Ask the children to read Chapters 3 and 4 independently. Explain that as they read, you want them to try to consider the story from the monster's point of view.

## During reading

**(C)** *(Summarising)* Talk with the children about the storyline so far. With whom do their sympathies lie?

**(C)** *(Prediction)* Ask the children to work with a talk partner to discuss what the monster might be about to tell Victor in Chapter 5.

## Independent reading

**(C)** *(Clarifying)* Now ask the children to read Chapters 5–7, asking them to notice how the monster is feeling.

**(V)** As children read, ask them to find vocabulary that describes the contrasting emotions that the monster has to deal with. They should notice that when he begins to feel secure he uses positive vocabulary. As soon as he sees his own reflection or is faced with his own face he uses negative vocabulary. Children may like to draw a picture of the monster and write the contrasting vocabulary on either side of it.

Frankenstein

**Assessment** Check that children:
- *(R, AF2)* can select the words and phrases from the text that reflect the monster's emotions.
- Ask the children to read to the end of the book independently. Ask them to try to identify the moral of the story as they read. Explain that they need to draw conclusions about why Victor's creation developed the personality of a monster. Would he have become a monster if Victor had displayed affection towards him?

## Returning and responding to the text

**Objective** Understand underlying themes, causes and points of view (7.2).

**C** *(Clarifying)* Having read the story, ask the children what they think the monster meant when he said 'Cruelty taught me to be cruel' (page 33, line 4). How does this line reflect the moral of the story? Ask the children whether they can think of other examples in stories in which someone's behaviour changes because of how they are treated.

**C** *(Clarifying)* Talk with the children about the phrase 'don't judge a book by its cover'. Discuss what they understand the meaning to be. How might this phrase apply to this story?

- Why do the children think that Frankenstein treated his monster so cruelly?

**Assessment** *(R, AF3)* Do the children understand that the monster reacts in the way that he does because he is seeking companionship and love?

## Speaking, listening and drama activities

**Objective** Improvise using a range of drama strategies and conventions to explore themes such as hopes, fears and desires (4.1).

**C** *(Questioning)* Revisit the end of Chapter 4. Ask the children, in pairs, to go into role as Victor and the monster.

- Invite the children who are playing Victor to ask the monster questions about how he behaves and why. Encourage the children role-playing the monster to explore how the monster was only looking for a friend.

## Writing activities

**Objective** Use different narrative techniques to engage and entertain the reader (9.2).

- Discuss how the children felt when they went into role as the monster and Victor.
- Remind them of the language and style of diary entries.
- *(Imagining)* Ask them, as the monster, to choose one significant moment in the story and write a diary entry about it. Encourage them to use some of the vocabulary they collected when they read the story.

**Assessment** *(W, AF1, 7)* Can the children write imaginative, interesting and thoughtful texts? Can they use effective vocabulary?

### Whole class reads
#### Books on a similar theme:
- *Strange Case of Dr Jekyll and Mr Hyde* by Robert Louis Stevenson
- *The Elephant Man* by Christine Sparks

### Cross-curricular links
#### Citizenship
- Using circle time, encourage the children to talk about how their actions affect themselves and others, to care about other people's feelings and to try to see things from other people's points of view. Talk about how the story of Frankenstein's monster might have been different if Frankenstein had been able to understand the monster's feelings.

#### Science
- Explore how a small amount of electricity can be generated using natural objects, e.g. lemons.

# Jane Eyre

**Author:** Charlotte Brontë (1816–1855)

**Synopsis:** Orphan, Jane Eyre, lives with a cruel aunt and spiteful cousins who, after mistreating her, send her to Lowood School. Thanks to the caring headmistress, Jane prospers at Lowood and secures a job as governess in Mr Rochester's Thornfield Hall. She falls in love with Rochester and they plan to marry until she discovers that he is already married and his insane wife lives in his house. Jane flees and by chance is taken in by kindly cousins of her father's family. One night Jane hears Mr Rochester calling to her. When she finds him she discovers his wife is dead and they are free to marry.

**Social and historical context:** The story is set in the north of England, sometime in the first half of the nineteenth century. During this time, the choice of school was decided by social class and gender. Jane Eyre was a penniless but bright orphan from a good family and yet considered of low social standing. Boys and girls were taught separately and children of poor or working class families were taught in local schools, such as the one in which Jane Eyre became a schoolmistress. These children would rarely progress beyond learning basic skills, most of the children would have left school by their early teen years to work on farms or in factories. Conditions in these schools were often as harsh as those depicted in Lowood Institution in *Jane Eyre*.

**C** = Language comprehension   **R, AF** = Reading Assessment Focus
**V** = Vocabulary enrichment   **W, AF** = Writing Assessment Focus

# Group or guided reading

## Introducing the book

**(C)** *(Prediction)* Look at the front cover and draw the children's attention to the style and nature of the house in the background. Then draw their attention to the illustration of the woman. What can they deduce about the two? What do her clothes suggest about what her position might be in the house? Look again at the picture of the house. Do the children notice the light on the top floor? How might this be significant? Ask the children to draw conclusions about the time period in which the book is set.

## During reading

- Read Chapters 1 and 2 together.

**(C)** *(Imagining, Questioning)* Go into role as young Jane as she sits alone in the 'red room'. Encourage the children to ask you questions about how you feel, why you are treated so badly by your cousins and aunts and the servants.

**(C)** *(Clarifying)* Ask the children to compare the experience of Jane in these chapters with those of a child in modern times. Are there any similarities or differences? Discuss how Victorians had different attitudes towards children and that because of poor health, there were often extended families who looked after family members.

## Independent reading

- Explain to the children that you would like them to focus on how telling the story in the first person helps to reveal the character of Jane. How much do we know of Jane's thoughts compared with others? Ask them to consider how the story might be different if it were told by another character such as her Aunt, Mrs Reed.

- How does the language and style of the text compare with contemporary literature?

**(V)** Ask the children to collect vocabulary specific to the time period. When they have collected a word, encourage them to write it on a small Post-it note to display for the rest of the class to see.

**Assessment** Check that children:
- *(R, AF5)* explain and comment on the writer's use of language, including literary features.
- Ask the children to finish reading to the end of the story independently.

### Returning and responding to the text

**Objective** Compare how writers from different times and places present experiences and use language (8.3).

**C** *(Summarising)* Ask the children to recap the main points of the story so far. What sort of girl is Jane? You might want to go into role as Jane and get children to explore the nature of her character. How did she become orphaned? How did she feel at the end of the story?

**C** *(Clarifying, Imagining)* Point out that the first person narration allows readers to know what Jane is thinking and feeling. Look at pages 36 and 37. What did Jane think of Mr Rochester? How did their first meeting make her feel? Help the children to notice how Bronte often uses the narrative form to express how Jane is fëeling about situations and people.

- Ask the children, in pairs, to go into role as Jane and Mr Rochester, thinking carefully about body language and facial expressions. When you give a signal, ask them to freeze in a position and encourage the rest of the group to comment on their pose.

**Assessment** *(R, AF5)* Can the children explain and comment on the writer's use of language?

## Speaking, listening and drama activities

**Objective** Improvise using drama strategies and conventions to explore themes such as hopes, fears and desires (4.1).

**C** *(Imagining)* Ask the children to return to the freeze frame they posed previously. Explain that you would like them to begin to carry out a dialogue between Jane and Mr Rochester. Remind them to use some of the vocabulary from the 'echo game'.

Jane Eyre

- Invite some children to act out their dialogue in front of the other children. Help them to evaluate each other's performances in terms of formality and choice of vocabulary.

## Writing activities

**Objective** Select words and language drawing on their knowledge of literary features and formal and informal writing (9.4).

- Re-read Chapter 27 (pages 81–83) with the children.
- Ask the children to write a chapter following on from this one that describes what happens to Mr Rochester from his point of view. Ensure they select appropriate vocabulary for the style, tone and time period, and follow the style of the author by writing descriptive compound and complex sentences, interspersed with dialogue.

**Assessment** *(W, AF7)* Can the children select appropriate and effective vocabulary to reflect the time period?

### Whole class reads
#### Books on a similar theme:
- *Rebecca* by Daphne du Maurier
- *Wuthering Heights* by Emily Brontë

### Cross-curricular links
#### Citizenship
- Ask the children to work in pairs to consider what makes a good relationship, thinking in particular about their own good friends. Together, ask them to list all the characteristics that make them a true friend. Invite them to write a 'recipe' for a strong relationship.

#### History
- To help children compare the differences between modern and Victorian homes, invite them to draw a picture of a room in a modern home, then label all the items in the room that have changed over time.

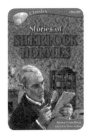

# Stories of Sherlock Holmes

**Author:** Arthur Conan Doyle (1859–1930)

**Synopsis:** In *The Boscombe Valley Mystery*, John Turner kills his blackmailer, Charles McCarthy, to prevent McCarthy's son, James, from marrying his daughter and claiming all of his property. In *The Adventure of the Blue Carbuncle*, Sherlock Holmes foils Mr Ryder's plans to steal a precious jewel and frames a plumber, John Horner, for the crime. *The Adventure of Silver Blaze* tells of how a trainer, John Straker, tries to injure his horse in order to win a bet, but is killed when the horse fights back! In *The Adventure of the Copper Beeches*, a selfish father, Jephro Rucastle, traps his daughter, Alice Rucastle, so he will not lose her money. His plan is foiled when his daughter's love rescues her.

**Social and historical context:** During the Victorian Age, writers often published novels serially, in weekly or monthly parts. Conan Doyle kept his readers coming back for more by creating the focus on a central character rather than on an ongoing plot.

Differences in class structure and living conditions of British society are clearly reflected in Conan Doyle's stories. London was a world centre of industry and commerce during the nineteenth century, and there was a clear divide between the rich and poor in society. Sherlock Holmes represented the ideal gentleman – someone who achieved respect through his own merit and talents.

---

**C** = Language comprehension    **R, AF** = Reading Assessment Focus

**V** = Vocabulary enrichment    **W, AF** = Writing Assessment Focus

# Group or guided reading

## Introducing the book

**C** *(Prediction)* If possible, try to bring in a deerstalker hat, a newspaper report of a crime and a large magnifying glass. Ask the children whether these artefacts suggest any particular character. Discuss whether they have ever heard of Sherlock Holmes. Read the blurb on the back cover of the book. Ask each child to predict what one of the mystery stories might be about.

## During reading

- Explain to the children that you will be asking them to write their own Sherlock Holmes adventure when they have finished reading the stories. They will need to focus carefully on the language and style of the stories. They will also need to notice how the stories are structured. Are there particular ingredients that Holmes uses in every story?

**C** *(Clarifying)* Read the first story, *The Boscombe Valley Mystery*, together. Ask the children to consider what the main ingredients are for the story. What is the key event or trigger? How are the chapters structured?

- Notice the sentence style that Doyle uses. Can the children use the sentences as a model to create a sentence of their own?

**V** Ask the children to collect examples of vocabulary that reflect the time period, to use later in their own Holmes story.

## Independent reading

- Ask the children to choose one of the other Sherlock Holmes stories to read independently. (Ensure that each story in the book will be read by at least one member of the group.) As they read, ask them to compare their story with *The Boscombe Valley Mystery*. Does it have a similar structure? Is the language style similar? Has the author used the same ingredients?

**Assessment** Check that children:
- *(R, AF6)* can identify and comment on the writer's style and language.
- *(R, AF4)* can comment on the structure of the text.
- Ask the children to read the remaining stories in the book independently.

### Returning and responding to the text

**Objective** Appraise a text quickly, deciding on its value, quality or usefulness (7.1).

**C** (*Summarising*) Ask individual children to summarise briefly the story they read for the rest of the group. Discuss which of the stories they preferred, encouraging the children to justify their decision.

**C** (*Summarising*) Ask the children to create a story map for one of the stories and then share it with a partner. Can they identify any particular structure that Doyle uses in his stories?

**Assessment** *(R, AF4)* Can the children comment on the writer's purpose for using a particular structure in the story?

## Speaking, listening and drama activities

**Objective** Use the techniques of dialogic talk to explore ideas, topics or issues (1.3).

**C** (*Questioning*) Go into role as Sherlock Holmes. Explain to the children that there has been a new murder discovered in the local area. Encourage the children to ask questions that would help them to write the story of the murder.

## Writing activities

**Objective** Use varied structures to shape and organise text coherently (10.1).

- Explain to the children that you have been asked by a magazine to create a new Sherlock Holmes style murder mystery.

- Recap the main features and structure of Conan Doyle's stories. Remind them of their story maps as a means of planning the story.
- Ask the children to plan, draft and edit a new story that could be sent to the magazine. You might want to encourage some of the children to include images and sound effects to create an online story.

**Assessment** *(W, AF3)* Can the children plan and write stories following the structure of a Sherlock Holmes' story?

## Whole class reads
### Books on a similar theme:
- *A Beautiful Place for a Murder* by Berlie Doherty
- *Whodunnit? Utterly Baffling Detective Stories* by Philip Pullman

## Cross-curricular links
### Citizenship
- Talk with the children about laws that they are aware of relating to crime. Discuss what might be appropriate punishments if people break these laws.

### History
- Explore crime, law and order during Victorian times by asking the children to find out what they can about 'Peelers' – the world's first police force. They could use the Internet to research and then present a short fact file about Peelers and their origins.

# Wuthering Heights

**Author:** Emily Brontë (1818–1848)

**Synopsis:** As children, Catherine Earnshaw and Heathcliff are inseparable but Catherine later rejects the dangerous Heathcliff to marry respectable Edgar Linton. When Linton puts an end to Catherine and Heathcliff's friendship, Catherine becomes ill and then dies in childbirth. Heathcliff seeks revenge by wooing Edgar's sister, Isabella, and cheating the Earnshaws out of their family homes. The story ends when the ghost of Catherine comes for Heathcliff and he dies, leaving the homes to their rightful owners.

**Social and historical context:** The story is set in Yorkshire, England, mainly during the late eighteenth century. Emily used the local moorland and valleys, and typical stone architecture, as the setting for *Wuthering Heights*. Illness and death were common occurrences during Emily's lifetime. Emily Brontë's older sisters, Maria and Elizabeth, died of tuberculosis before they were fifteen, and in *Wuthering Heights*, Edgar and Linton also die of wasting diseases.

---

**C** = Language comprehension  
**V** = Vocabulary enrichment  
**R, AF** = Reading Assessment Focus  
**W, AF** = Writing Assessment Focus

---

## Group or guided reading

### Introducing the book

**C** *(Clarifying)* Talk with the children about the North Yorkshire Moors in Emily Brontë's time period. Discuss how wild it might be living up on the moors.

**C** *(Imagining)* Read up to the end of page 7 to the children. Ask them to try to visualise the room of the house where Mr Lockwood has arrived. What would it look and smell like? What sounds would there be?

## During reading

**(C)** (*Clarifying*) Ask the children to read the rest of Chapter 1. As they read, ask them to note down the names of each of the characters they meet on a sheet of paper. Once they have read the chapter, help the children to begin to interpret the relationship between the characters. Can they draw lines between the characters' names to show how they are linked?

**(C)** (*Prediction*) Can the children predict who the ghost might be?

**(C)** (*Questioning*) Ask the children to think of one question they might like to ask Hareton Earnshaw.

**(V)** Focus on the last line on page 12, when Mr Lockwood says he 'was feeling as weak as a kitten'. Why do the children think the author has chosen the kitten reference? What other similes can children think of for feeling weak?

**(C)** (*Prediction*) Read to the end of Chapter 2 together, and ask children to predict what the rest of the story might be about. Some children might like to go into role as Nelly Dean – Mr Lockwood's servant – and tell their own versions of the story ending.

## Independent reading

**Objective** Understand underlying themes causes and points of view (7.2).

- Ask the children to read up to the end of Chapter 5 independently and to continue adding information to show the relationships between the different characters.

- (*Imagining*) Encourage them to consider the story from Heathcliff's point of view. Where might he have disappeared? How might he feel when he visits Cathy again?

- (*Clarifying*) Ask the children to review the characters they identified. Can they discuss how they are linked, backing up the information with evidence from the text?

Wuthering Heights

**Assessment** Check that children:
- *(R, AF3)* can infer how the characters are linked
- *(R, AF2)* can use evidence in the text to back up their opinions about the relationships between the characters.
- Ask the children to finish reading to the end of the story independently.

### Returning and responding to the text

- **(C)** (*Clarifying*) Ask the children to draw conclusions about why Heathcliff married Isabella.

- **(C)** (*Summarising*) Discuss the character traits of Heathcliff. What sort of man do the children think he is?

- **(C)** (*Summarising*) Ask the children to consider the impact of having two narrators – how does this affect the story and the pace? Why do they think the author chose Nelly Dean as the main narrator?

**Assessment** *(R, AF3)* Can the children draw conclusions about the character of Heathcliff and give reasons for his actions?

## Speaking, listening and drama activities

**Objective** Consider examples of conflict and resolution, exploring the language used (3.1).

- Ask the children to choose one of the following roles to assume: Nelly, Linton, Cathy, Hareton or Heathcliff. Encourage the children to carry out a discussion in role to explore the actions of the individuals. How could they have acted differently?

## Writing activities

**Objective** Use different narrative techniques to engage and entertain the reader (9.2).
- Recap the story with the children. Ask the children whether they have read any other stories that feature ghosts – tragic or otherwise.

- Ask half of the group to draw a picture of a male character, while the other half draw a female character. Encourage the children to make up powerful names for the characters.
- Using the pictures and names, ask the children to match a male character with a female character.
- Now ask them to draw a picture of a setting. Shuffle the setting pictures and give a picture to each pair of children.
- Using the setting and the two characters, ask the children to compose orally a tragic ghost story. Once they have prepared the story, invite them to tell it to another pair.
- Finally, allow the children to write their own version using one, or a combination of the two stories they have heard. Remind them of the structure of *Wuthering Heights*, where flashbacks of events witnessed by Nelly Dean are given.

**Assessment** *(W, AF1)* Can the children write an imaginative story, following the structure used by the author?

## Whole class reads
### Books on a similar theme:
- *Girl in the Attic* by Valerie Mendes
- *White Peak Farm* by Berlie Doherty

## Cross-curricular links
### Geography
- Talk with the children about where the story is set. Ask them to find descriptions of the moors and the climate of the area, e.g. '...the entire countryside was now one mass of white billowing snow' (page 12). Encourage the children to research books and the internet to find pictures of moorland, especially the North Yorkshire Moors, in different seasons. How is this environment similar or different from where they live?

### History
- Ask the children to find out information about one disease that had a huge impact on life in the eighteenth century, e.g. smallpox, typhus, tuberculosis. Can they find out why the disease may no longer be a threat to society today? How did the disease affect life in the eighteenth century?

# Treasure Island

**Author:** Robert Louis Stevenson (1850–1894)

**Synopsis:** When an old pirate dies in his parents' inn, Jim Hawkins takes possession of a treasure map, and with Dr. Livesey and Squire Trelawney, he sets sail to find the treasure. When he discovers that the ships' crew, led by Long John Silver, plan to mutiny and steal their treasure, Jim has to work hard to outwit the pirates. Eventually, Jim and his friends triumph and return to England with their share of the treasure, but not before the slippery Long John silver has escaped, taking four hundred guineas with him.

**Social and historical context:** Pirates were both feared and romanticized as heroes. They thrived on the booty they stole from merchant ships and shoreline villages.

Stevenson, born in Edinburgh, wrote *Treasure Island* in 1881. The idea for his story came when, on holiday in Scotland, he and his stepson drew and coloured an imaginary 'Treasure Island' map.

Stevenson's father and grandfather were both lighthouse engineers and frequently took young Robert Stevenson with them on their travels. Long John Silver is based on Stevenson's friend, writer and editor, William Henley, who lost his lower leg due to tuberculosis of the bone.

Victorian England was a vast empire and had the largest navy in the world. Stevenson crossed the Atlantic two years before he wrote *Treasure Island*.

 = Language comprehension   **R, AF** = Reading Assessment Focus
 = Vocabulary enrichment   **W, AF** = Writing Assessment Focus

# Group or guided reading

## Introducing the book

**(C)** *(Prediction, Questioning)* Build excitement on the subject of pirates and treasure, by placing a treasure chest in the classroom for the children to discover. Generate questions with the children: Whom might the chest belong to? What type of person might it belong to? Do children know anything about pirates? How could they find out whom it belongs to?

- Ask the children to read up to page 16 independently. As they read, encourage them to consider who the author is.

## During reading

**Objective** Understand how writers use different structures to create coherence and impact (7.3).

**(C)** *(Clarifying)* Discuss who the narrator of the story is. Why do the children think the author chose Hawkins to be the narrator? What do they notice about the language style?

- Read Chapters 16 and 17 together. Why do they think the author decided to change the narrator for this section?
- What impact does this have on the storyline?
- How do the different viewpoints of the narrators alter the story?

**(V)** Ask the children to gather vocabulary linked to the subject of pirates and sailing. They could then use the vocabulary in their writing activity

## Independent reading

- Ask the children to read to the end of the book independently. As they read ask them to pay particular attention to who the narrator is in each chapter.

**Assessment** Check that children:
- *(R, AF4)* can identify the impact of different narrators on the story.

## Returning and responding to the text

**C** (*Questioning*) Ask one of the children to take on the role of Long John Silver, and encourage other children to ask him questions.

**C** (*Imagining*) Ask the children to imagine how the story might have been different if Long John Silver had been telling it.

**C** (*Clarifying*) Invite the children to draw conclusions about why Long John Silver behaves the way he does. What might have happened in his past? How does he get on with people? What events in his life might have shaped the way he is?

**Assessment** *(R, AF4)* Can the children imagine how the story might have been different if it had been told by Long John Silver?

# Speaking, listening and drama activities

**Objective** Make notes when listening for a sustained period and discuss how note-taking varies depending on context and purpose (2.1).

- Explain to the children that they are going to use visual symbols as a way of note-taking when listening to and reading sections of *Treasure Island*.
- Ask one child to read Chapter 1 aloud, then model to the children how you might use visual symbols as an aid in taking notes. Share with them ideas for possible symbols that might represent some of the key elements of the stories. Use the children's ideas to build a key that can be used to support their own visual note-taking. Discuss other sorts of notes they could use, such as writing key words, drawing a map, etc.
- Now ask children to read up to the end of Chapter 5. As they read ask them to make visual notes in their reading journals.
- Children could attempt to retell a chapter to a talk partner by referring to the notes they have made.

# Writing activities

**Objective** Use different narrative techniques to engage and entertain the reader (9.2).

- Ask the children what they learned about Long John Silver through hot-seating the character. How might the story be different if he had told it?
- Revisit sections of the story to remind the children about the style of the writer.
- Then focus children's attention on the vocabulary they have gathered about pirates and sailing.
- Ask the children to write the story from Long John Silver's point of view using the style of the original story.

**Assessment** *(W, AF1)* Can the children write from a different narrative point of view?

## Whole class reads

### Books on a similar theme:
- *Moonfleet* by John Meade Falkner
- *Pirateology* by Dugald Steer

## Cross-curricular links

### Geography
- Ask the children to use facts from the story to map the journeys of Jim Hawkins.
- Explore how coves are created by the action of waves.

### History
- Encourage the children to find out about explorers in the fifteenth to seventeenth centuries. (Each child might like to do some in-depth research on one explorer.) Why were there so many explorers? What impact have their explorations had on society today?

# Robinson Crusoe

**Author:** Daniel Defoe (1660–1731)

**Synopsis:** The story is the diary of Robinson Crusoe, shipwrecked on an island for 27 years. After living peacefully for 25 years on the island, cannibals visit the island. Crusoe rescues a captive whom he calls Friday. Together they rescue more captives: a Spaniard, and Friday's father who promises to help them escape to Europe. Before this help arrives though, Crusoe and Friday capture an English ship from mutineers and the captain takes them to England.

**Social and historical context:** At the beginning of the 1700s there were many real-life stories of castaways. Defoe was inspired by Andrew Selkirk who was a castaway for 4 years at his own request.

The story was written at a time when Britain dictated its own cultural values on nations within its empire. Crusoe is portrayed as a 'king' of the island, and the island is referred to as a colony towards the end of the novel. Crusoe and Friday are depicted as having a master/servant relationship. However, Crusoe's attitude towards slavery changes.

Defoe's religious beliefs as a Christian come through strongly in the story, upholding moralistic views above all else.

---

**C** = Language comprehension      **R, AF** = Reading Assessment Focus
**V** = Vocabulary enrichment       **W, AF** = Writing Assessment Focus

---

## Group or guided reading

### Introducing the book

 *(Clarifying, Prediction)* Ask the children if they have heard of this book. What do they already know about the story? If they have not heard of it, can they use the picture to deduce what the story might be about?

## During reading

**Objective** Compare how writers from different times and places present experiences and use language (8.3).

- Read up to the end of page 12 together. As they read, ask the children to identify language structures specific to diary entries, e.g. first person. How does the language reflect the time period?

**(C)** *(Imagining)* Read the entry for November 4th, 1659 to the children. Do not let them see the picture of the fortified camp on page 15. Ask the children to listen carefully and draw what they imagine the fortification to look like.

**(V)** Ask the children to skim through the book and write down vocabulary related to the nautical theme.

## Independent reading

**(C)** *(Clarifying)* Ask the children to read to the end of the book independently. As they read, ask them to focus on how writing in the style of a diary enables the writer to move the pace of the story on through the years. Ask them to notice how the writer marks the passage of time, organising the chapters as specific days. Can they identify how he moves the pace by deciding to write only on days when a key event takes place?

**Assessment** Check that children:
- *(R, AF4)* can comment on the author's structure and organisation of the text.

## Returning and responding to the text

**(C)** *(Clarifying)* Discuss the themes that the children thought were evident in the story.

- What were the good and bad things about living on the island?

**(C)** *(Summarising)* Ask the children to develop a compare and contrast grid, similar to that found on page 13 of *Robinson Crusoe*, to consider the pros and cons of living on a desert island.

**Assessment** *(R, AF3)* Can the children imagine what it would be like to live on an island?

# Speaking, listening and drama activities

**Objective** Participate in a whole-class debate using the conventions and language of debate, including standard English (1.2).
- Explain to the children that half the group will argue about why it would be wonderful to live on a desert island whilst the other half argue against this point of view. Explain that at the end they will decide whether Robinson Crusoe will spend the rest of his life on the island or not.

# Writing activities

**Objective** Use paragraphs to achieve pace and emphasis (10.2).
- Ask the children to think back on their own lives. Can they identify key points or significant events in their lives?
- Ask them to write one paragraph about each of those days in a diary, using the same techniques that the author used to move time and pace along.

**Assessment** *(W, AF3)* Can the children use the style and techniques of the author?

## Whole class reads
### Books on a similar theme:
- *Kensuke's Kingdom* by Michael Morpurgo
- *Plundering Paradise* by Geraldine McCaughrean

## Cross-curricular links
### Geography
- Ask the children to scan the book and make notes about the location of different points on the island. They could then draw a scale map of Crusoe's island.

### History
- Encourage the children to find out what the main trade routes were in Tudor times. Who were the most significant explorers? What were their boats like? Explore how boats have changed over time.